Looking at Countries

ETHIOPIA

Kathleen Pohl

FRANKLIN WATTS
LONDON • SYDNEY

First published in 2009
by Franklin Watts

Franklin Watts
338 Euston Road
London NW1 3BH

Franklin Watts Australia
Level 17/207 Kent Street
Sydney, NSW 2000

First published in 2009 by Gareth Stevens Publishing
1 Reader's Digest Road
Pleasantville
NY 10570-7000 USA

Dewey number: 917.3
ISBN: 978 0 7496 8250 7

Senior Managing Editor: Lisa M. Herrington
Senior Editor: Barbara Bakowski
Creative Director: Lisa Donovan
Designer: Tammy West
Photo Researcher: Charlene Pinckney
Reading consultant: Susan Nations, M.Ed.

Photo credits: (t=top, b=bottom, l=left, r=right, c=center)
Cover (main) © Robert Harding Picture Library Ltd./Alamy; Cover (inset) and title page © Tony
Waltham/Robert Harding World Imagery/Corbis; p. 4 Frances Linzee Gordon/Lonely Planet Images;
p. 6 © Martin Harvey/Alamy; p. 7t © Miglavs/Danita Delimont/Alamy; p. 7b © Franck
Guiziou/Hemis/Corbis; p. 8 Ariadne Van Zandbergen/Africa Imagery; p. 9t Boris Heger/
AP; p. 9b © Tony Waltham/Robert Harding World Imagery/Corbis; p. 10t © Trevor Smithers
ARPS/Alamy; p. 10b © Jon Arnold Images Ltd./Alamy; p. 11t © Gavin Hellier/JAI/Corbis; p. 11b
© Images of Africa Photobank/Alamy; pp. 12–13 © Sean Sprague/Alamy; p. 14t © Robert Harding
Picture Library Ltd./Alamy; p. 14b Chris Fairclough/CFW Images; p. 15 © Friedrich Stark/Alamy;
p. 16 Frances Linzee Gordon/Lonely Planet Images; p. 17t © Robert Preston/Alamy; p. 17b
© Andrew Holt/Alamy; p. 18 Chris Fairclough/CFW Images; p. 19t © Viviane Moos/Corbis; p. 19b
Jonathan Alpeyrie/Getty Images; p. 20l © Keith Levit/Alamy; p. 20r John Dominis/Time Life Pictures/
Getty Images; p. 21 Manoocher Deghati/IRIN; p. 22 © Wolfgang Kumm/dpa/Corbis; p. 23t
© Andy Chadwick/Alamy; p. 23b © Richard Human/Alamy; p. 24 © Borderlands/Alamy; p. 25t © David
Gray/Reuters/Corbis; p. 25b © Puchinger/imagebroker/Alamy; pp. 26–27 Shutterstock (3)
Every attempt has been made to clear copyright. Should there be any inadvertent omission please
apply to the publisher for rectification.

Printed in China

Franklin Watts is a division of Hachette Children's Books,
an Hachette UK company.
www.hachette.co.uk

Contents

Where is Ethiopia?

Ethiopia is a country in north-east Africa. It borders five other countries. Sudan is to the west, Somalia and Djibouti are to the east, Kenya is to the south and Eritrea is to the north.

Did you know?

Ethiopia and its neighbours make up the Horn of Africa. This area has a shape like the head and horn of a rhino. Look at the map. Can you see the horn?

EUROPE

AFRICA

Indian Ocean

Atlantic Ocean

ETHIOPIA

N
W E
S

Ethiopia is bordered by both smaller and larger countries.

The kings who once ruled Ethiopia loved lions. This lion statue is in a square in the capital city, Addis Ababa.

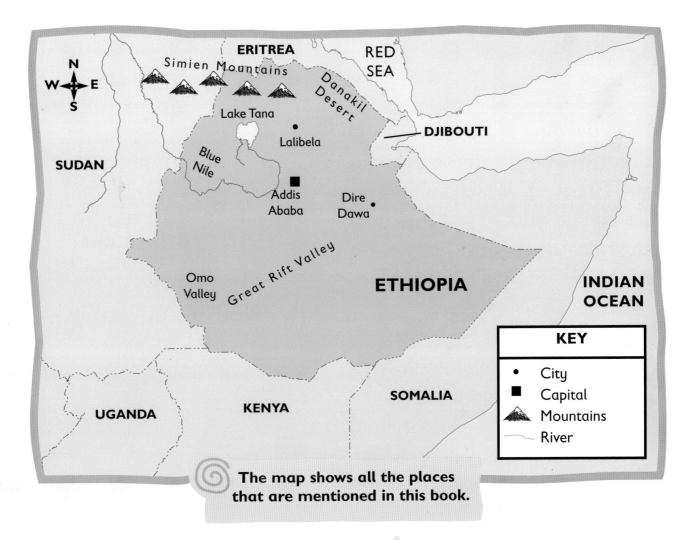

The map shows all the places that are mentioned in this book.

Ethiopia is close to both the Indian Ocean and the Red Sea. However, the country is land-locked which means it has no coastline. Goods in and out of the country usually pass through a neighbouring country, Djibouti.

Addis Ababa is the highest capital city in Africa. It sits on a plateau – a high, flat area of land. The city has grown in size without much planning. Modern buildings stand next to small mud and grass huts or tin shacks.

The landscape

The Ethiopian Plateau makes up about two-thirds of the country. The Great Rift Valley cuts through the middle of the plateau, from north to south. Most people live on the plateau as it has the country's best farmland.

Across the central plateau are lowlands, with grassy plains, forests and deserts. Wild animals such as rhinos, lions and jackals roam freely. Colourful birds live there, too.

Did you know?

The gelada baboon can only be found in the Ethiopian mountains.

The gelada baboon is a rare animal that lives in Ethiopia.

Ethiopia has mountains and volcanoes. The Simien Mountains in the north of the country have the highest peaks.

The longest river in Ethiopia is the Blue Nile. It flows from Lake Tana, the country's biggest lake. The Blue Nile feeds into the River Nile, which is the longest river in the world.

Termites, wood-eating insects, live in Ethiopia. Some termite nests are as tall as trees.

The Blue Nile Falls drop about 45 metres. In the rainy season, a cloud of mist hangs over them.

Weather and seasons

Most of Ethiopia has a warm climate. The hottest and driest area is the Danakil Desert, which gets very little rain. The highlands, where the most rain falls, have cooler temperatures. Some of the mountains even have snow on them.

Did you know?

The Danakil Desert is one of the hottest and lowest places on Earth.

These are salt beds in the Danakil Desert. People mine the salt and sell it.

Heavy rainfall can leave roads and bridges under water. The floods can make life very difficult.

Some areas of Ethiopia are covered in dry grassland.

The country's rainy season lasts from June to September. Ethiopian people call it the 'big rains'. Winds called monsoons bring heavy rainfall and floods.

Ethiopia also has years when no rain falls at all, causing droughts and famines. In the 1980s, around 900,000 people died because there was not enough to eat.

Ethiopian people

More than 76 million people live in Ethiopia. It is one of the poorest countries on Earth and it is also one of the oldest. Kings ruled at least part of Ethiopia for almost 2,000 years.

Did you know?

In 2001, scientists dug up the bones of an early human ancestor. The bones, found near Addis Ababa, were more than five million years old.

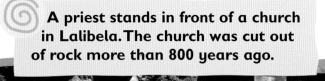
A priest stands in front of a church in Lalibela. The church was cut out of rock more than 800 years ago.

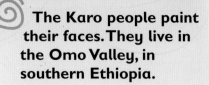
The Karo people paint their faces. They live in the Omo Valley, in southern Ethiopia.

This girl has woven colourful bread baskets.

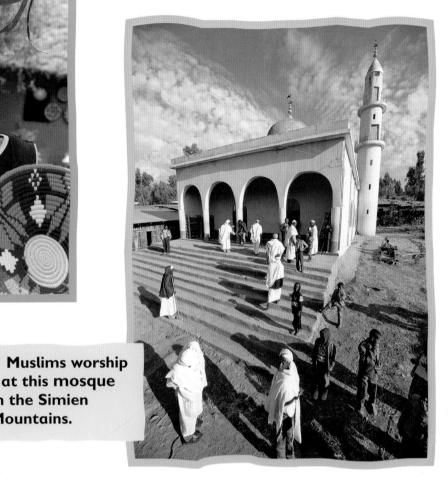

Muslims worship at this mosque in the Simien Mountains.

People from 80 different ethnic groups live in Ethiopia. The biggest groups are the Oromo and the Amhara. Each group of people has its own language and way of life. Sometimes the groups fight each other. This type of fighting is known as civil war.

Most Ethiopians are Christian or Muslim. The main language of the country is Amharic. Many Ethiopians speak English, which is taught in schools.

School and family

State school is free in Ethiopia. However, only about six or seven out of every ten children go to primary school. In the past, few girls were sent to school but the number of girls in school has doubled in the past few years.

Many schools are very poor. There is little money for books and teachers. One teacher may have as many as 70 students.

Two children study their books. In some places, lessons are held outdoors.

In this classroom, students sit at desks to do their schoolwork.

An Ethiopian family stands in the doorway of their home.

In the first classes, children study history, Amharic, English and maths. Few pupils finish primary school as their parents need them to help on family farms.

Most families have several children. The father is usually the head of the house while the mother cooks and cares for the family. Many girls marry when they are very young.

Did you know?

In Ethiopia, many girls do not choose their own husband. Their parents make that choice.

Country

Most Ethiopians live in the countryside on small farms or in tiny villages. Often villages do not have electricity or clean drinking water. Many people die young from disease.

This woman is collecting water from a village pump. Few homes in the countryside have running water.

Some villages are just small groups of huts.

A lot of farmers struggle to feed their families and have little left over to sell. A grain called teff is the main food crop. Farmers also grow corn, wheat and coffee beans.

Children work in the fields. They chase birds away from the crops and they look for firewood. Many children help to care for goats, sheep and chickens.

Most farmers in Ethiopia are too poor to own modern farm machines. They use oxen to pull wooden ploughs.

In the desert, people called nomads move from place to place. They look for good areas to find food and to graze their animals.

Did you know?

Deserts have spread over land in Ethiopia that was once good for growing crops.

City

In Ethiopia, about one in every five people lives in a city. In recent years, more people have moved to the cities to look for work. Many houses there have electricity and running water. There are also more schools and better healthcare.

Did you know?

Ethiopia does not have any ports. Goods are shipped in and out of a port in nearby Djibouti.

People at the railway station in Addis Ababa. There are few railway lines in Ethiopia.

Blue-and-white van taxis are familiar sights in the city.

These women shop at an outdoor market in Addis Ababa. The market is the largest in Africa.

Addis Ababa is Ethiopia's biggest city. It is home to more than two million people. This busy city has office buildings, banks and shops. It is famous for its large outdoor market. The second-largest city is Dire Dawa, a major centre of trade. It lies along the railway route between Addis Ababa and Djibouti.

Most people who live in the cities do not own cars. They walk to work, ride motorbikes or take buses or taxis.

Ethiopian homes

In the country, many houses are made of dried mud, straw and sticks. They have thatched roofs, which are made of grass or straw. Most houses are circular, with only one room. In the north, some people live in stone houses.

Did you know?

Some Ethiopians bring their goats and sheep into their huts at night. This keeps them safe from wild animals that might hunt and eat them.

Most huts are round and have thatched roofs. The roofs slant to help the rain run off.

Nomads take their homes with them as they move from place to place. Camels carry the tents made of animal skins.

In the city, some rich people live in big houses. Others live in tall blocks of flats. Poor people live in grass huts or tin shacks, with no water or electric lights.

Cities have tall blocks of flats, houses and huts – where the poorest families live.

Many people became refugees as they fled the war between Ethiopia and Eritrea.

Some people in Ethiopia are refugees. They have left other countries to escape danger, such as war. They live in huts or tents in crowded camps.

Food

Most people in Ethiopia grow the food they eat. They cook over a fire and eat one or two hot meals a day. The main food is *injera*, a kind of flatbread made from teff. People eat it with spicy stews made from meat and pulses.

Did you know?

Injera takes the place of plates, forks and spoons. It serves as a big plate for spicy stews piled on top. People tear off small pieces of injera to scoop up the stew.

A woman cooks injera over a fire. The flatbread looks like a giant pancake.

A typical breakfast may include *wat* and injera. Wat is a stew made of chickpeas.

In the cities, people buy fresh fruit and vegetables at outdoor markets.

Many Ethiopians also make bread from the root of the *ensete*, a type of banana plant. They eat boiled barley and roasted corn, too. They also grow potatoes, cabbages, beans and mangoes to eat. Some people raise sheep, goats and camels for meat.

Many Ethiopians drink *tej*, a wine made from honey. They also drink coffee, tea and a thin, sour yogurt drink.

Wars and droughts in the last 30 years have often caused food shortages. Many Ethiopians have died because there was not enough food to eat.

At work

Most people in Ethiopia work on their own small farms or on huge farms called plantations. The government owns the plantations where the main crop is coffee. Coffee is a cash crop, a crop grown to be sold, not eaten by farmers. Other farm products include sugar cane, livestock and beeswax.

Did you know?

Experts think coffee first came from Ethiopia. The beans grow wild in some places there.

In the cities, some women work outside the home. These workers are sorting coffee beans by hand.

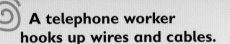

A telephone worker
hooks up wires and cables.

This nurse works
at a health clinic.

Some people work in factories
in cities. Factory workers
make cloth, cement, leather
and shoes. Ethiopia trades
goods with other countries,
including the UK.

In cities, many people work in shops, restaurants,
banks or offices. Some are doctors or nurses.
Others work for the government. A few people
fish or work in the country's gold mines.

Having fun

Most people in Ethiopia do not have much time for fun. Still, some Ethiopians enjoy playing sport. They like football and *ganna*, a type of hockey. People play basketball, volleyball and tennis in cities that have courts. Some ethnic groups have their own sports. Stick fighting is a popular sport in south-western Ethiopia.

Girls have fun playing a game of football after school.

Did you know?

Some of the best long-distance runners in the world have come from Ethiopia. Both men and women have won Olympic medals.

This marathon runner won a gold medal at the 2004 Olympic Games in Athens, Greece. His name is Kenenisa Bekele.

Adults like to play chess, cards and a board game called *gabata*. Children enjoy listening to folk tales. They play games that are a lot like hopscotch and hide-and-seek.

Most holidays in Ethiopia are religious. People go to special services. They also enjoy feasts, parades and music.

Every year, people celebrate Timkat. This is a three-day Christian festival.

Ethiopia: the facts

- The official name of Ethiopia is the Federal Democratic Republic of Ethiopia. It became a federal republic in 1994.

- The president is the chief of state, or formal representative of the country. The prime minister is the head of the government.

- Ethiopians who are 18 years old or older may vote.

- Ethiopia is not often at peace. Sometimes its people are at war with one another. At other times, Ethiopia is at war with its neighbours, including Eritrea, Sudan and Somalia.

- Eritrea used to be part of Ethiopia. Eritrea gained its independence from Ethiopia in 1993. A long war followed.

The flag of Ethiopia has three colour bars of green, yellow and red. At the centre is a blue circle with a five-pointed star.

Ethiopia's unit of money is the **Birr**.

Lions with black manes are also called Abyssinian lions. Only male lions have black manes.

Did you know?

The lion is the symbol of Ethiopia. The country is famous for its lions with black manes. Many of them once roamed free in Ethiopia. Today only about 1,000 of the lions live in the wild.

Glossary

Ancestor family member who lived in the past.

Birr the unit of money in Ethiopia.

Chief of state the formal representative of a country.

Civil war a war in which people in the same country fight each other.

Drought when a region does not get any rain for a long time.

Ensete a plant that belongs to the banana family. Ethiopians use the roots to make flour for bread.

Ethnic groups groups of people with the same cultures, traditions and ways of life.

Famines great shortages of food.

Federal republic a system in which the national government and the states have separate powers. Elected officials represent the people.

Gabata an Ethiopian board game.

Ganna a game played in Ethiopia that is similar to hockey.

Injera the main food of Ethiopia, a flatbread made from teff.

Jackals wild dogs with large ears, long legs and bushy tails.

Land-locked not bordered by water on any side.

Livestock farm animals such as cows, goats and sheep.

Monsoons seasonal winds that bring heavy rains.

Mosque a Muslim place of prayer and worship.

Nomads people who move from place to place, living in tents and grazing their animals.

Oxen the full-grown males of domestic cattle, usually used to pull loads on farms. Oxen are slow-moving but very strong.

Plantations very large farms on which crops such as cotton, tobacco, sugar cane and coffee are grown.

Plateau a high, flat area of land.

Refugees people who flee their country, often for political or religious reasons.

Teff a tiny, round grain used to make flour for bread.

Thatched made of bundles of grass, palm leaves, or straw.

Find out more

http://news.bbc.co.uk/cbbcnews/hi/newsid_4090000/newsid _4096800/4096880.stm
The BBC Newsround guide to Ethiopia. You could also follow links to their section on Africa.

http://travel.nationalgeographic.com/places/countries/ country_ethiopia.html
The National Geographic magazine on-line guide to Ethiopia.

Note to parents and teachers: Every effort has been made by the Publishers to ensure that these websites are suitable for children, that they are of the highest educational value, and that they contain no inappropriate or offensive material. However, because of the nature of the Internet, it is impossible to guarantee that the contents of these sites will not be altered. We strongly advise that Internet access is supervised by a responsible adult.

Some Ethiopian words

There are 83 different languages spoken in Ethiopia. Amharic is the official language used by government and in school. It is written using a different alphabet to our own.

Speak some Amharic:

English	Say...
hello/bye	teanaste'lle'n
I'm fine	ene dehna nene
see you	chow
yes	awo
OK	e'shi
no (not true)	ie
thank you	amesege'nallo'
excuse me	yike'rta
sorry	aznallo'
my name is	semo man nuw

My map of Ethiopia

Trace this map, colour it in and use the map on page 5 to write the names of all the towns and cities.

31

Index